Original title:
The Brooch's Quiet Story

Copyright © 2025 Creative Arts Management OÜ
All rights reserved.

Author: Vivian Laurent
ISBN HARDBACK: 978-1-80586-030-3
ISBN PAPERBACK: 978-1-80586-502-5

Stories Held Close

In the drawer where secrets sleep,
A little pin with tales to keep.
It once adorned a hat so grand,
Now it sits, a lonely band.

Whispers shared in pockets tight,
It sparkles softly, catches light.
A party hat for cats and mice,
Dances a tune, oh how nice!

Dancers in Dull Light

Once upon a time, it shone,
At a gala all alone.
It joined a tie in a grand ball,
But tripped instead, just made us fall.

In the back, where shadows play,
It giggles on a rainy day.
A little laugh, a wink, a jest,
Worn on coats, it feels the best.

Curated Chaos of Moments

Tangled in a yarn of dreams,
In chaos, creativity beams.
A splash of flair on socks worn thin,
Spinning stories with a grin.

Caught in laundry's fray and fold,
Adventures whispered, yet untold.
It dreams of parties, wild and free,
A dash of fun for you and me.

Reflections of a Life Adorned

On a jacket, it took flight,
Glinting bravely in the night.
A quirky charm from days of yore,
Each shimmer holds a tale in store.

It may be chipped, or lost a gem,
Yet still it stands, a little hem.
With every glance, a chuckle's found,
In humble glory, laughter's crowned.

Captured Whispers of Tomorrow

In a drawer where secrets hide,
Sparkling tales of joy abide.
Each tiny clasp a giggling friend,
As little moments twist and bend.

Laughter stitched in golden lace,
A golden pin with a silly face.
It holds the fabric of our fun,
A circle round, a loop unwound.

Tiny dancers in a line,
Wobble, giggle, intertwine.
Each gem a wink, each loop a song,
Whispers echoed all along.

The tales they weave are quirky, bright,
Funny pin that brings delight.
In each shimmer, stories ring,
Tomorrow's laughs on tiny wings.

Echoing Threads of Truth

A silken thread holds laughter tight,
Beneath the gleam, a playful sight.
Secrets shared with every clip,
A funny twist, a curvy trip.

With sparkles bright, it starts to hum,
Whispering jokes, a soft, fun drum.
Each tiny catch a teasing jest,
Threads of truth, they never rest.

A tiny charm with quirk and cheer,
Holds memories of laughter near.
In every wink, a story's glow,
Echoes of joy in every show.

Through fabric folds and time's embrace,
Funny tales hold their rightful place.
As moments pass on silver threads,
It tells the tales that laughter spreads.

Glimmering Geometries of Time

Circles spin in a polished dance,
Each shiny angle sparks a chance.
Triangles nod and squares behave,
Crafting giggles, little waves.

A diamond's cut, a laugh unframed,
Geometry games, never tamed.
Spinning stories in every fold,
Glimmering truths that never grow old.

Rhombus, ellipse, all spin around,
Time's humor lost, then found.
Every point conceals a grin,
In the geometry, we all win.

From point to line, and back again,
Life's funny shapes, a playful pen.
In every curve, a joke is made,
Glimmering paths that never fade.

The Threads of Wear and Care

A twist and turn, some threads unravel,
In the seams, let's laugh and travel.
Each little snag tells a tale,
Of morning mishaps, silly fail.

Worn and torn, the fabric sings,
Funny memories, the joy it brings.
Each little fold holds laughter's flair,
In wear and care, let's boldly share.

A little pin, a party guest,
With every pin, it's always dressed.
It winks and giggles while it stays,
Threads of laughter in funny ways.

Through all the bumps and gentle pulls,
Sewing smiles, it gently rules.
In every pin, a cozy joke,
Threads of wear, and laughter woke.

An Ornament's Silent Song

Upon my coat, a shiny pin,
A steadfast friend with echoes thin.
It winks at folks who stroll on by,
With secrets shared—no need to pry.

In pockets deep, it finds its space,
A little laugh, a silly face.
It jests of journeys, tales untold,
With whispers made of gleaming gold.

The cat takes aim, it hits the floor,
A dance of chaos—oh, what a roar!
Yet, somehow, it comes back around,
To twinkle bright without a sound.

So here we twirl, in silly glee,
An ornament's song, just you and me.
No grand ballads, just some fun,
An artifact, but who's the one?

Jewel's Embrace

Once upon a shirt that's neat,
A cheerful gem found on a seat.
It giggles softly, clinks and clatters,
As friends and foes share wild patters.

In between the crumbs and crumbs,
It glistens bright, but oh, it hums!
With every poke and little prod,
A quirky laugh, a funny nod.

When someone plops it on too tight,
It squeals a giggle—what a sight!
A laughter trapped in jeweled bars,
Dancing light like little stars.

So if you find this jewel so bold,
Just know its stories all unfold.
With every twist, its tales expand,
An unexpected friend at hand.

Echoes of Where We've Been

In dusty drawers where memories sleep,
A shiny tale begins to peep.
It whispers softly, plays coy games,
Reminding us of quirky names.

There's Timmy's dance, there's Laura's shoe,
Each moment pinned and held anew.
With every glance, a chuckle stirs,
Oh, the capers and the blurs!

Once on a pet but now misplaced,
How silly life feels, ever laced.
With mischief wrapped round every loop,
It tells of joy, of friend-filled soup.

So let us cherish these funny days,
While echoes of laughter swirl and sway.
This tiny gem, though worn and gray,
Still twinkles bright in its quirky way.

Crafting Memories in Clarity

Nailed to a cork or lose on a spree,
This little charm tells tales with glee.
Once on a hat that blew in the breeze,
Now hides in pockets, at ease with tease.

It winks to every tale we sow,
Of coffee spills and high school shows.
Remember when it saved the day?
Or danced the night young hearts did sway?

A mishap here, a slip of fate,
A brooch that laughs, who can relate?
With every memory, buttoned tight,
Jokes interlaced in day and night.

So as we wander this vibrant scene,
Let memories glow, and laughter glean.
In simple pieces, joy is found,
With every sparkle, love abounds.

Whispers of Adornment

A pin so small, with tales to tell,
It dances lightly, casting a spell.
In pockets deep, it likes to hide,
While secrets wiggle, full of pride.

From lady's coat to gentleman's hat,
It plays a role, like a cheeky cat.
A glint of gold, a wink of lace,
Embracing mishaps with a smiling face.

The party starts, and off it goes,
To join the fun, where laughter flows.
It catches crumbs and whispers true,
"This evening's wild! What shall we do?"

A badge of honor, of grace and glee,
In every twist, a memory.
So here's to pins, delightful and bright,
They weave the tales of our delight!

Elegance in Silence

In velvet boxes, them we keep,
A treasure trove, while we hope and leap.
With glittering eyes, they softly muse,
In sparkling silence, they refuse to snooze.

At fashion shows or cozy nights,
They steal the spotlight, all the rights.
With sneaky smiles, they bolt away,
Turning old shirts into grand display.

A tiny wink, a subtle grace,
They add to charm, a friendly face.
In clumsy hands, they laugh along,
Who knew that brooches could be so strong?

With tales of laughter, they twirl and spin,
In every gathering, the vibe they win.
So here's to moments that laughter brings,
And the silent grace that a pin can sing!

Shine of Forgotten Charms

Nestled away in drawers so deep,
They giggle softly as secrets seep.
Though times have changed, and styles, too,
They peek out shyly, saying, "Look at you!"

Gathering dust with stories to share,
They sparkle softly, without a care.
In funky shapes, they waddle and sway,
Reminding us of a splendid day.

Once the life of many a dance,
Now contemplate their second chance.
A rogue revival, a retro spree,
With every twinkle, they scream, "Yippee!"

Take them out, give them a spin,
Rediscover the joys they bring within.
In each forgotten charm, a laughter stays,
A glimmer of light in mundane days.

Secrets Beneath the Surface

Under layers, whispers swirl,
A little secret, waiting to twirl.
In pockets hidden, mischief brews,
This simple pin has tales to choose.

They wear the emotions of April's glow,
With glances bold, while time creeps slow.
A sassy wink at the midnight hour,
As laughter blooms from this little flower.

Hitching rides on jackets and tees,
They charm us all, with playful tease.
Each clasp a giggle, each hook a grin,
What stories would surface, if they could begin?

Wrapped in silence, so aptly bright,
In every fold, there's pure delight.
Let's celebrate these tiny sparks,
For they hold the joy of countless larks!

Precious Moments Encapsulated

In shadows cast by glittering light,
A tale unfolds, a spark in sight.
Pinched laughter, secrets held tight,
Whispers of joy in the moonlight.

A clasped smile on a tiny bird,
It chirps a tune, though none have heard.
Stitches of time, laughter interred,
This little gem, forever stirred.

A sparkle caught on a playful breeze,
Tickling hearts with tidbits that tease.
A memory wrapped in laughter's ease,
Mirth in moments, life's little keys.

Adventurous tales of olden days,
Worn on blouses, a thousand ways.
Each glimmer spins in vibrant plays,
Tickling fancies in sunlit rays.

Treasures from Yesterday

Old trinkets hide with a merry grin,
Treasures of laughs thick as thieves win.
Crisp petals, where do we begin?
With a wink and a nod, let's dive in!

Jumble of stories, so funny and bright,
Where laundry mischief inspires delight.
The colors clash, but all feels right,
Dancing in shadows until the night.

From dusty corners, they often peek,
Encouraging smiles, a little cheek.
With every glance, a playful tweak,
At memories stored, the heart feels weak.

Buttons and bows, a patchwork of cheer,
Tailor-made giggles, so near, so dear.
Each wrinkled tale rises, clear,
Transporting us back to yesteryear.

Layers of Meaning

A pearl of wisdom, wrapped in sass,
Beneath the surface, joys amass.
Tiny tales can be a big laugh,
Layers of meaning in a dainty craft.

Quirky patterns, each stitch a joke,
Lively drama woven in choke.
As we unfold, we all invoke,
Guffaws that scatter like flavored smoke.

With every twist, a story untold,
Memories gathered, colorful and bold.
Frolicsome squabbles that never grow old,
In the fabric of life, treasures unfold.

Adornments with giggles, just take a glance,
Each layer a partner in life's swirling dance.
Time spins and twirls, in a lively prance,
Once lost in laughter, we all take a chance.

The Timeless Weight of Beauty

A whimsical weight rests on the heart,
In playful humor, we each take part.
Jokes stitched together, a charming art,
Glimpses of grace where laughter can start.

Forgotten mementos with quite the twist,
Remind us of moments we dare not miss.
Each glance draws a laugh, a little tryst,
A beautiful chaos, who could resist?

Light at the seams, where stories collide,
In daydreams of whims, we all can reside.
Fables of joy grow round with pride,
In soft laughter's grip, we can abide.

Fleeting moments, like sparkling dew,
Fables of friends entwine in a crew.
With every chuckle, the world feels new,
The timeless weight stems from laughter's view.

Beneath the Sparkle

In a box of shining wonder,
Sits a gem with tales to tell.
It sparkles like a gossip maven,
Winks when worn, oh what the hell!

Once a lady's grand possession,
Now it feels so out of place.
Dusted off for a dinner,
Brooch, you've got quite the face!

You're a glimmering quick-witted,
Every glance just makes you grin.
With each smile, a story's knitted,
Who could guess the mishaps in?

Beneath the flair and shimmer bright,
Lies a history, oh so bold.
Charmed by whims in the limelight,
From fancy balls to young and old.

The Conversation in Carats

Once a chatty citrine gem,
Spoke to sapphire, bold and blue.
"Listen here, my dazzling friend,
What crazy things we've been through!"

They joked of days in evening gowns,
When hearts would skip with every twirl.
"Remember that, in all our crowns?
I outshone that clumsy pearl!"

With each laugh, their settings sparkled,
Setting off a comedic show.
Rubies chimed, their glee unparkled,
"Oh please, who will steal the show?"

Caught in a light of snappy banter,
Gems unite, their legacies sing.
With every jest, a glow, a canter,
Endless joy in a setting bling.

Tales Adrift in Luminous Metal

In corners of a dusty drawer,
Lay tales wrapped in golden thread.
Each twinkle whispers 'once before,'
In laughter's warmth, they never fled.

They danced with grace at every glance,
Making mischief in throngs of guests.
With every dinner and romance,
Oh, the trouble those gems bequeathed!

Adrift in tales like ships at sea,
Set sail on nights that felt so fine.
They wore their humor playfully,
A history that loves to wine.

In gleaming settings, humor glows,
As memories tickle through the night.
With every shine, the laughter flows,
Embracing past with pure delight.

Echoes of Past Elegance

In grand halls where echoes linger,
Gemstones sparkled with such flair.
Whispers of elegance, light as a finger,
Dragging laughter through lavish air.

Once at a ball, a prance gone wrong,
A loop-de-loop that stole the night.
"Oh dear, was that a toe you stepped on?"
Gems chuckled, their sparkle bright!

Travelers of time and space,
They still recall a lively jest.
In settings bold, they hold their place,
Creating joy, they never rest!

Through mirror's glint, the past is clear,
Echoes of whimsy, never shy.
In polished tales, you'll always hear,
Laughter's glow, it won't say bye.

Layers of Meaning

A sparkly jewel on a lapel,
Faded tales it has to tell.
Whispers from a long-gone trend,
Tangled threads that twist and bend.

Once a gift from Auntie Sue,
Or maybe just a prize or two.
With each notch and every groove,
A timeline of the life it proved.

Pin it on a drunken night,
Fish out stories, laugh in spite.
Who knew that old piece could cause,
Such a ruckus, such a pause?

As it gleams against the light,
Shining tales from left to right.
In the end, just plain old fun,
Its journey's lost, but not the pun.

Glints of the Unseen

A little glimmer, oh so sly,
Hiding secrets with a wink and sigh.
Caught in cracks of yesteryears,
Spilling laughter, mixing tears.

In the attic, a dance of dust,
Finding treasures we can trust.
Unraveled laughter, tales untold,
Glints of mischief, brave and bold.

Stitched with stories of romance,
Who picked it up? A fateful chance.
Grabbed once by a dog named Fred,
Now on a shelf beside my bed.

So here it sits, this trinket bright,
Making mischief day and night.
A little jester, cheeky, spry,
With every glint, it winks, oh my!

Narrative in Metal

A metal tale that spins around,
Secrets woven, humor found.
Tiny stories latch on tight,
Poking fun, making delight.

Once upon a hurried race,
In a cupboard, a hidden place.
Clinks and clatters of the past,
Tales that tickle, sure to last.

Fastened on a winter coat,
It narrates a life afloat.
Each button's tale and hook's embrace,
Makes us chuckle, just in case.

With every flash, a jest reveals,
Life's quirks and silly wheels.
In every shine, a tale so merry,
This narrative is light and cheery.

A Hidden Legacy

Buried deep in a velvet case,
A relic with a silly face.
Hilarity wrapped in old design,
Glimpse at history, oh, how divine!

Once worn proudly at a dance,
Spinning stories with a glance.
Forgotten now, in dusty halls,
A legacy that chuckles and sprawls.

From a quirky grandparent's hand,
To this curious, comic land.
Each angle holds a tiny jest,
A legacy that laughs, no less!

Polished bright, it teases fate,
Winking as it radiates.
A hidden gem, forever free,
Such humor in its mystery!

Silent Baton's Melody

In twilight's glow, a baton sways,
Engaging in its silent plays.
It winks at stars, with secret airs,
Conducting chuckles, mingled flares.

As shadows dance beneath the moon,
A symphony of laughter's tune.
Each twirl and twist, a giggle sparks,
While giggling blooms in hidden parks.

The whispers wrap 'round gathered folks,
Who snicker softly at the jokes.
With every sway, the stories tease,
Echoed laughter carried by the breeze.

In this warm night, all cares demand,
Are two left feet and a clumsy hand.
So join the tune, let spirits rise,
In silent melodies packed with surprise.

Luminous Lingers of the Past

An old mirror grinned, with secrets deep,
Reflecting tales that make one leap.
It winks and nods, with a cheeky air,
As memories flit, like lightest flair.

A jaunty hat from yesteryears,
Shimmies forth, as laughter appears.
Its feathered plume's a ticklish tease,
Tickling minds like a teasing breeze.

The clock's hands play a funky game,
For each tick-tock has a quirky name.
Time tiptoes with a giggly zeal,
Bouncing moments, surreal reveal.

In playful shadows of crisp delight,
The past unfolds, a hearty bite.
So dance and prance with wild delight,
In luminous whispers, day turns night.

Refined Textures of Memory

A tapestry spun with threads of fun,
Woven tales that dance as one.
Each fiber hums a timeless jest,
With colors bright, they jest and fest.

Lace of laughter interlaces life,
Borrows joy from trivial strife.
Each stitch a wink, a twinkle bright,
Making memories, pure delight.

Fancy frills whisper in the breeze,
Poking fun at such trivial keys.
The fabric folds, a comical play,
Where silly patterns lead us astray.

So grab a piece of this fancy weave,
And wear your quirks, you'll soon believe,
In textures bold, where laughter thrives,
A party of joy, where memory survives.

A Touch of the Timeless

In a pocket, a trinket stirs,
Winks at time, as laughter purrs.
With a grin, it has tales to share,
Of clowns and jesters, quirks laid bare.

A dainty charm with an age-old spin,
Whispers softly of where it's been.
Each little touch holds quirky spins,
Stories that tumble, tailored grins.

With every pluck, it surely sings,
Of silly antics and joyful flings.
In timeless tones, it tickles the mind,
Leaving echoes of laughter left behind.

So embrace that charm, let it play,
In your heart, it will convey,
A cosmic joke on fate's rehearsed stage,
A touch of timeless, a laugh-filled page.

The Art of Holding Moments

A shiny pin on a jacket's lapel,
Winks as it catches the light so well.
It holds tight to secrets of laughter and tears,
Sharing its tales through the passing years.

It wobbles and jiggles with every dance,
Mocking the whims of a fleeting glance.
Each twist and turn a story to tell,
With sparkle and charm, it wears them so well.

From grandmas to kiddos, it holds all the dreams,
Each gem on its surface just silently beams.
It's seen all the moments, both funny and bright,
And sways in delight under soft candlelight.

So cherish the trinkets that sit on the shelf,
For they hold the history of you and yourself.
Each pin's like a button, so silly and spry,
In a world full of noise, it simply sighs and flies.

Decorative Testaments

A bejeweled critter, perched on a dress,
With eyes that twinkle, oh what a mess!
It grins from the fabric, in wild relief,
Reminding us all of mischief and grief.

Each season it winks with a glow just right,
Claiming its story in the dead of night.
With every occasion it gives a sly wink,
Making us ponder and pause to rethink.

From teas to the dinners, it knows the score,
It giggles and whispers of what came before.
A flamboyant flower, a rascal in gold,
Telling our tales, both raucous and bold.

Let's toast to the treasures that tickle the eye,
With laughter and joy, they flutter on by.
For in every sparkle, a lesson unfolds,
In this mishmash of life, it laughs and it scolds.

Hidden Narratives of Bling

A charm on a chain, a glimmering sprite,
It grins at the world, ready for a fight.
From first dates to blunders, it prides itself,
While resting and lounging next to dusty bookshelves.

It tells stories of dates that went quite askew,
Of tripping on heels and spilled soda too.
With every shine, it chuckles along,
Keeping our secrets with a whimsical song.

Each gem a chapter, each sparkle a laugh,
Sketching our lives like a doodler's draft.
In pockets and purses, it dances to be,
The unsung hero of our history.

So raise your glasses to memories worn,
To trinkets that make us feel light as dawn.
In the quirky tales of the past that it brings,
We find all the joy that a funny heart sings.

When Trinkets Speak Softly

Whispers from earrings, bold on display,
Share laughter and folly in their own way.
Delicate chains shiver like leaves in the breeze,
Carrying echoes that tickle and tease.

Each pendant has quirks, each bracelet takes flight,
In the world of the mundane, they bring sheer delight.
Jewels that giggle, with stories to share,
They dance on our skin, spreading joy everywhere.

For parties and picnics, they dress up the day,
Laughing at life's little slips and foray.
Draped in our moments, they keep us afloat,
In the sea of the serious, they're the fun little boat.

So cherish the baubles that playfully twine,
For they know how to sparkle, shimmer, and shine.
In laughter and love, they softly remind,
That joy can be found in the brightly designed.

The Hidden Heart of Accessories

Underneath the clasp and pin,
A secret life begins within.
A lady's whims and daily grind,
In shiny metal, tales unwind.

A paperclip once on a spree,
Joined a brooch for a cup of tea.
Beneath the surface, laughter flows,
In quiet corners, mischief grows.

A Glimmering Tapestry of Tales

In a drawer filled with dust and dreams,
Lies a necklace bursting at the seams.
It whispers tales of long-lost fun,
Of singed hair and baking in the sun.

Each bead a giggle, each charm a cheer,
A story shared back when we'd steer.
Through laughter and chaos, they've survived,
Bundled together, jests contrived.

The Language of Lost Lusters

Once a spark in a lady's draw,
A wild earring broke the law.
It danced and twirled like it was free,
Chasing crumbs of sweet jubilee.

With a wink, a wink, it shared its grace,
A whispering jest in an empty space.
For every twist, there's a chuckle nearby,
In the romance of lost luster, say goodbye.

An Unseen Narrative

In the shadows of an old hat box,
Rest stories hidden like sneaky fox.
A rogue button laughs at its fate,
While clipped ribbons gossip, so great!

With each flicker in a dimmed light,
Earrings bicker until the night.
An unseen narrative unfolds so sly,
In the tick of time, chirps the shy.

Stories That Glitter

A little trinket on the shelf,
It winks and sparkles all by itself.
Once held a secret, oh what a tale,
About a cat who danced with a whale.

In the drawer, it starts to hum,
Of all the parties and pies that crumb.
A fashion statement, quite absurd,
It makes me giggle, what a silly bird!

It dreams of days when it wore a crown,
Dazzled all in the small town.
But now it sits, just faking flair,
Telling jokes to the bathroom air.

Oh, stories wrapped in shiny charms,
With history's quirk and all its harms.
Let's raise a glass to tales unwound,
And laugh at treasures we have found.

Adornments of Personal Myth

A charm that whispers 'I've been around',
Worn on a blouse, where laughter's found.
It told of giants who lost their hats,
And dances with frogs wearing tiny spats.

Each time it jangles, it shares a jest,
Of funny moments, it loves the best.
Once kissed a prince, or so it claims,
Now it's stuck with my messy frames.

At parties, it struts in glittery pride,
While the stories inside it refuse to hide.
It giggles softly with every sway,
Creating gaffes in a cheeky ballet.

These tales we carry, each a delight,
In pearls of wisdom, we gleefully write.
Under the starry, whimsical night,
It vibrates with laughter, oh what a sight!

Gentle Hues of Heritage

A pin of blue, the shade of skies,
Hides a history, with twinkled eyes.
It snickers softly, sharing its cheer,
About those socks that made quite the smear.

Grandma wore it to a wild dance,
A story of youth and mischievous chance.
The other pins just rolled their eyes,
While she twirled 'round with teasing sighs.

Once it tamed a wild and woolly head,
Invited the chaos to come and spread.
It chuckles still, in its gentle hue,
Sharing secrets 'twixt the old and new.

With every glance, it starts to glow,
Unraveling laughs we've yet to know.
Heritage wrapped in laughter's embrace,
Creating memories no time can erase.

Secret Histories in Silver

A silver clasp conceals a grin,
Spinning yarns of ups and downs within.
It gossips tales of a soiree fate,
When cupcakes fought and everyone ate.

Oh, the mischief it always leads,
Whispers secrets of forgotten deeds.
Laughing at moments when hats went askew,
A comical dance, just me and you.

The locket seems to snort and chuckle,
As it recalls the great puddle struggle.
Each sparkle holds a wink of lore,
A tiny adventure you can't ignore.

With every twist, its charm is clear,
It's a merry trinket, let's draw it near.
Let's toast to laughter, tales revive,
In silver echoes, our joys arrive!

Secrets Woven in Metal

In a drawer, it hides and waits,
Twinkling tales of silly fates.
Captured whispers, made of lace,
A dance of echoes in one small space.

Dancing with the socks so bold,
It's heard more jokes than I am told.
The stories woven, oh what a twist,
Like grandma's laugh, you get the gist.

With a flick, it flashes bright,
Its shimmering grin, a pure delight.
Telling secrets, just for fun,
When fashion's over, it's still number one.

So here's to it, our cheeky friend,
In style, it knows just how to blend.
With every twinkle, a laugh unspun,
A gem of humor, never overdone.

Silent Sentinels of Grace

Perched atop varied seams so neat,
Guarding stories, oh so discreet.
A steadfast laugh, in silence veiled,
Through uptown luncheons, it prevailed.

It witnessed drama, had a front row seat,
As socks mismatched and shoes felt beat.
Inquiet moments, it held the glee,
Of spilled coffee shared by you and me.

When fashion trends swing left and right,
It chuckles softly, a comical sight.
In corners quiet, it keeps its place,
A keeper of quirks, with subtle grace.

So here's to the gems that whisper shy,
In the realm of style, they dare to fly.
With every heartbeat, a hidden embrace,
Through laughter and tales, in splendid space.

Stories Embedded in Gemstone

Buried deep in a velvet box,
A glimmer of laughter next to old socks.
Each gem a giggle, each stone a quirk,
Ready for mischief and fun to work.

Caught in a bounce, a far-flung twirl,
Polished to shine, give it a whirl.
A tumble here, a trip over there,
Those tiny stones? They don't have a care!

Crafted wisdom, brightened by cheer,
Each facet holds a joke, oh dear!
In the dance of fancy, a tale unfolds,
With every statement, a new story told.

Let's raise a toast to sparkle and shine,
To playful wonders, forever entwined.
For laughter is timeless, and gems find their way,
In a world where chuckles are here to stay.

A Quiet Elegance Unfolds

Nestled soft, a secret plays,
In quiet elegance, it strays.
Whispered giggles threaded tight,
In the shadows, pure delight.

A twinkling nod, a wink of gold,
With stories shared, never old.
Twisting tales, through fingers dance,
Making laughter a fashion's chance.

So let it shine, our little delight,
In all the chaos, it sparks the light.
A feathered wink, a sly charade,
Through colors bright, it won't evade.

From silly moments to moments grand,
It shares a laugh, it takes a stand.
In beauty's grace, it finds its jest,
A charm of humor, forever blessed.

An Antique's Embrace

In an attic high, treasures piled,
A cat with a hat, looking quite wild.
A trinket sparkled, all dusty and grand,
Whispers of how it once sat in hand.

How it curtsied in royal shows,
While hidden from ghosts of long-ago foes.
Its laughter echoed, a twinkle in time,
Every glance at it, a whimsical rhyme.

A dance with the past, a flip of a coin,
Tales of adventure from places it's known.
With secrets that giggle, it tells of its years,
Brightening moments with laughter and cheers.

Wrapped in nostalgia, it winks with delight,
Bringing smiles to faces, both day and night.
An antique's embrace, a treasure to seek,
In every small laugh, its history speaks.

Reflections in a Pin

A shiny little pin, with a story to tell,
It glimmers and shimmers, but don't ask it well.
For when it was fancy, a true fashion star,
It once held together a gown from afar.

In musing it dreams of those wild galas,
Of slips on the carpet and toes in the balas.
It chuckles at mishaps, the pins and the pricks,
Everyone's laughter, it savors and picks.

To tiny notes pinned on a collar so sweet,
A love note forgotten beneath someone's seat.
It winks at the whispers, the hints it has heard,
A mirror of memories, each giggle occurred.

And every reflection comes chasing its light,
Each moment is captured, a pure delight.
In pin's little heart, joyful stories reside,
With winks and small chuckles, they dance side by side.

Heartbeats of Heirlooms

Old pendant swinging, it sways with a grin,
Whispers of love lost and laughter within.
Once worn at the dances where giggles took flight,
Now it snoozes away, dreaming day and night.

Its heart, a soft thump, remembers the scene,
Of zany relatives and costume queen.
Oh, how they twirled in sequined delight,
Under the glimmering disco ball's light.

With each bead it breathes, a pulse of old fun,
From birthdays and picnics under the sun.
It plays in nostalgia, the jester in gold,
Telling hilarious tales that never grow old.

In the drawer it hums, to no one it speaks,
But on weekends it dances while everyone shrieks.
These heirlooms with heartbeats find joy in their past,
With laughter and love, forever amassed.

The Alchemy of Attachment

A charm on a bracelet, a wiggly thing,
It promises journeys, oh, the joy it can bring.
From pockets and purses, it's traveled the scene,
Gathering stories where no one has been.

Each trinket it bears, a memory tight,
Of friends who exchanged them one whimsical night.
There's a rubber band bouncing, a button gone rogue,
Whispering how it once danced on a toad's leg like a yolk.

In the dance of attachment, each tale fills the room,
From bumbles to tumbles, each heirloom's perfume.
They laugh in the corners where quiet things hide,
With chuckles and giggles, they snuggle inside.

A thimble's sweet sigh, a sock's playful tease,
It speaks to the threads, the moments that freeze.
The magic is real in the laughter we weave,
Crafting ourselves as we lovingly cleave.

Tokens of Memory

In a drawer tucked away, so neat,
A treasure rests that can't take heat,
With stories sewn in every pluck,
But all it does is sit and cluck.

Each pin and clasp, a giggling pout,
They tell of times when life's in doubt,
A clasp that's lost its shiny charm,
Yet still it hopes to work some harm.

A stolen glance and then a chuckle,
Memory's quirks make my heart buckle,
The tales they tell, all somewhat wild,
Of mishaps lived since I was a child.

Nostalgia drips but laughter sings,
From all the past and silly things,
These tokens hold their quiet fate,
In stitches that we dare not rate.

Stitches of Silence

A button lost, it laughs a lot,
In silence found, it draws a plot,
A thread that tangled, just for fun,
It's shy but knows it's number one.

Each stitch a giggle, every knot,
They weave a tale, but it's forgot,
Secured with love but loose with tales,
In quiet seams, the humor prevails.

A safety pin, a jester grand,
It knows the secrets never planned,
With every poke, it wears a grin,
The quiet tales of where I've been.

In fabric's fold, the stories sprout,
Between the laughs, we twist about,
Stitches shy that softly plead,
In silence found, they plant their seed.

Adrift in Antique Allure

In boxes hid, with dust to claim,
A charm that giggles at its fame,
Like ships adrift in memory's sea,
With anchors made of laughter, free.

Each curve and angle, whispers bright,
They twinkle back with sheer delight,
A mustard yellow, a plaid old flair,
Hiding secrets, it doesn't care.

Polished once, now quite the fuss,
It rolls around, thinks it's a plus,
In corners dark, the stories creep,
Where antique dreams refuse to sleep.

Each lipstick stain, a joke retold,
In fancy light, it sparkles bold,
Adrift we stream with laughter's glow,
In antique allure, the memories flow.

A Glimmer in the Shadows

In shadows deep, a shimmer hides,
A wink of mischief, nowhere bides,
A glimmer caught by wandering eye,
Telling tales that make you sigh.

From every corner, laughter peeks,
Through glints of gold and rusty creeks,
Each tiny spark, a comic jest,
In tales that never dare to rest.

A laughing pin, with stories cheeky,
Lurking there—oh so sneaky,
In pockets deep, they chase the light,
With stories told in sheer delight.

A fluttered heart, a chuckle flares,
What's found in shadows, no one cares,
A glimmer shows what's often missed,
In laughter's glow, we can't resist.

Silence of the Shine

In a drawer where wonders dwell,
A shiny gem begins to tell.
With every twist and every turn,
It laughs at secrets, sly and stern.

A glitter here, a shimmer there,
It conjures tales without a care.
An absent-minded fashion craze,
That steals the spotlight in strange ways.

A glance reveals its cheeky grin,
It knows just when to let folks in.
With sparkling eyes, it shares a laugh,
Of fashion faux pas on its behalf.

In whispers low, it tells the truth,
Of pointy hats and poodle poof.
Behind each sparkle, giggles hide,
A jovial gem, with nothing to bide.

Threads of Time's Embrace

Threads woven with tales of yore,
Time's laughter echoes, evermore.
A tangled yarn, a jumping jest,
It tickles fancies with its best.

A stitch from back when fashion bloomed,
With quite the style that was presumed.
Knick-knacks laugh in every phase,
Remembering the silliest days.

With colors bright and shades so bold,
Each twist spins stories, truths retold.
An old sock claims it was the star,
Of disco nights, a dancing czar.

Around it swirls a jaunty breeze,
Threads of laughter, oh how they tease.
A garment's giggle, a vintage flair,
It keeps on spinning tales to share.

Gems Whisper Secrets

Gems in a case, all in a row,
Holding secrets from long ago.
A ruby winks, a sapphire grins,
It's all a game where laughter begins.

A diamond twinkles with delight,
It whispers truths through day and night.
With playful nudges, it softly hints,
At wild parties and silly flints.

It's not just shine that draws the eye,
But echoes of fun that never die.
One gemstone chuckles, "What a dance!
Those funky shoes, what a chance!"

Past lives giggle in colors bright,
Crafted of joy, spun with light.
Adventures buried in shimmering hues,
A carnival of memories to amuse.

Adornments of Memory

Adornments placed on chests of gold,
Invite the memory to unfold.
From grandma's pearls to granddad's tie,
Each piece a joke, a wink, a sigh.

A locket laughs, "Do you recall?
That time we danced, we had a ball!"
Worn with pride or left in haste,
They paint our lives in even taste.

A bracelet jests about lost shoes,
Of summers spent in playful snooze.
With every clasp, a chuckle shared,
Of fleeting moments, slightly bared.

These treasures sing in soft delight,
Reminding us of purest light.
They wear the tales of yesteryears,
Bringing us smiles along with tears.

A Pin's Tale of Time

In a drawer of gems and sparkly things,
A pin once danced with all the bling.
It wiggled here, it giggled there,
Telling tales of days beyond compare.

Once upon a scarf, it took a ride,
Twisting tales with every slide.
A butterfly pinned to a suit so neat,
It whispered secrets to the feet.

A safety pin held together dreams,
While fashion faux pas became their creams.
It chuckled softly, a wild delight,
In rags and riches, it sparkled bright.

So give a cheer for the little pin,
Who shares the laughs, the losses, the win.
With every poke, a smile it brings,
A tiny ruler of shiny things.

Embers of Elegance

A sparkly gem lost in the fray,
Winks at the world in a cheeky way.
With each occasion, it finds its flair,
Turning drab to fab with little care.

Draped on a dress, it twirled in fun,
Whispering tales of how it won.
At parties galore, it twinkled with glee,
The queen of quirk, all eyes on thee!

Once it saved a shirt from fate so dire,
Stitching together a look that's fire.
With humor in placement, it danced anew,
Charmed all who glimpsed its dazzling view.

So here's to the bling that loves to play,
A beacon of laughter and sass every day.
In the laughter of elegance, it always sings,
A riot of color, in the joy it brings.

Echoes of Lost Moments

Once tucked away in a cabinet tight,
A pin recalls a dance late at night.
It chuckles softly, a wink of cheer,
Keeping the memories ever near.

It held together a wild affair,
A sneaky fastener, unaware of care.
Lost in the wash, found on the floor,
Each twist and turn became folklore.

A jester of fabric, a playful stuck,
Bringing whimsy with every pluck.
From formal wear to pajamas untamed,
It finds a way to be forever famed.

So here's to the echoes that never fade,
Crafted from laughter, memories made.
In every fold and crinkle, it glees,
This pin of moments, a treasure with ease.

The Art of Subtle Grace

A tiny pin rests with casual flair,
Whispering secrets in the air.
With barely a nudge, it plays its part,
An elegant waltz from the very start.

It holds together a queen's old gown,
Turning frump to fab without a frown.
With a wink and a jig, it knows the score,
Making fashion history, never a bore.

A mischief maker, it hides in plain sight,
Intriguing whispers, glittering bright.
With every button, it waves goodbye,
To dull and dreary, oh my, oh my!

So raise a toast to the pin of grace,
The sneaky hero with a playful face.
In the tapestry of trends, it leaves a trace,
The art of fun in its subtle embrace.

The Brocade's Soft Confession

In a drawer so neat and snug,
Where secrets hide with threads that tug,
A tale of laughs in silk entwined,
Of whims and dreams that crossed the mind.

Each strand a giggle, a twist of fate,
With colors bright, they dance and wait,
To tickle thoughts and start a cheer,
In whispers soft, they pull quite near.

A tangled mess, but oh so sweet,
A patchwork quilt of funny feats,
For every stitch a chuckle shared,
A memory stitched, a heart ensnared.

So here we find, in folds and seams,
A symbol of our silliest dreams,
With laughter sewn into the fray,
A brocade's charm in life's ballet.

Mementos of Light

In corners dim where memories gleam,
A playful glint, a beam's wild dream,
They dance upon the table's edge,
With stories bound in laughter's pledge.

A flash of jest, a wink from fate,
Each little gem cannot await,
To spark a grin or raise a brow,
And tease the heart with joy's soft vow.

They jingle softly, bright and loud,
In gatherings where folks are proud,
A winking nod, a knowing glance,
In every sparkle, life's own dance.

So let them shine, those mementos bright,
In silliness, they find the light,
For every glimmer holds a tale,
Of laughter shared on joy's own trail.

Chasing Fleeting Glimmer

In fields of dreams, where shadows play,
A twinkle here, a wisp away,
With every chase, the giggles grow,
As sunlight bids the clouds hello.

A fleeting flash, a wink, a zoom,
In every corner, laughter blooms,
We chase the glimmers, oh so fleet,
In echoes of our quickened feet.

But glimmers fade, they slip, they slide,
Yet still we run, with hearts open wide,
For every laugh we hold so dear,
Turns moments lost into cheer.

So let them dart, those fleeting things,
In every joy, a silly sting,
We'll chase the light, where giggles form,
In every glimmer, playful, warm.

Shadows of Sentiment

In twilight's grip, where shadows sway,
A hint of joy will find its way,
With echoes low, they call and tease,
In every shadow, laughter's breeze.

The whispering shades tell tales of old,
Of moments bright and hearts so bold,
Where silliness wraps the night in glee,
And dances lightly, wild and free.

A playful poke, a cheeky smile,
In shadows cast, we linger awhile,
For with each giggle, time suspends,
In tender tales where laughter blends.

So let the shadows softly guide,
Through corners bright, where jesters hide,
In every sentiment, laugh and play,
For life's true joy is in the sway.

Whispers of Light and Life

Once pinned upon a shirt, so bright,
It told tales of laughter, took flight.
A clasped grin, a wink in its shine,
A little piece of joy, divine.

In gardens of fashion, it danced and spun,
Outshining friends, oh what fun!
It giggled with colors, played hide and seek,
In pockets of whimsy, it found its peak.

Caught between buttons, it chuckled aloud,
Making moments laugh, drawing a crowd.
Napping on coats, it dreamed of the trees,
While tickling hats in a gentle breeze.

With stories unraveled, between laughs it gleamed,
A tiny memento, the wildest it seemed.
It whispered of life, of joy and delight,
In a world full of tales, where all was bright.

Unraveled Tales

A sparkling tale with every glance,
Twisted in threads of a curious dance.
It nudged at the fabric, so ready to share,
Secrets of silliness, floating in air.

A mystery crafted, with a twist and a spin,
It chuckled with charm, where stories begin.
In pockets of time, it found its own rhyme,
A secret collector, so sweet, so sublime.

Like gossiping friends, on a blustery day,
Unraveled tales in a whimsical way.
With humor unkept, it sparkled and shone,
In worlds of fashion, it proudly roamed.

A treasure of laughter, a vintage delight,
In corners of closets, it danced through the night.
A golden reminder, of joy found in seams,
In stitches of stories, it wove silly dreams.

Guardians of Form and Fashion

In the kingdom of pins, it wore a crown,
Guarding its treasures, never a frown.
Draped in fabrics, it kept spirits high,
Clashing with styles, oh me, oh my!

A classy defender, of style and grace,
With a wink and a nod, it ran the race.
It giggled at collars, fluffed up sleeves,
While stitching the dreams of fashion thieves.

With a flash of its shine, it called for a toast,
To fabrics and threads, the thing that it loves most.
A maestro of laughter, in sequins it spun,
Uniting the threads, making style such fun!

Dancing with colors, a whimsical brat,
It turns heads at parties, in games of chitchat.
As guardians go, it wrapped hearts in cheer,
With fashion as joyful, as laughter sincere.

A Legacy Unclasped

With a pop and a wink, it loosened the chain,
A legacy swirling, in laughter's refrain.
From grandmas to daughters, they giggled with glee,
As stories of elegance spun free like a bee.

In a walk-in closet, a treasure trove grew,
Each clasp full of secrets, a fashion déjà vu.
It pranced through the years, with each twist and fold,
Revealing the wisdom of all it had told.

It twinkled with mischief, each shimmer a jest,
An heirloom of humor, the very best.
In gatherings rich, it started a cheer,
As nostalgia danced, and the past drew near.

From fabric to laughter, oh what a delight,
A legacy fun, in the moon's soft light.
In hearts it's still stitched, its stories intact,
A timeless reminder, of joy that's abstract.

A Touch of Timelessness

In a drawer so deep and wide,
Lies a pin with nowhere to hide.
A tale of laughter, lost and found,
Dances 'round in silence, profound.

Once it sparkled, oh so bright,
Now it giggles in the light.
Every twist has quite a jest,
Chasing fashion's silly quest.

With a clasp that's slightly loose,
It claims it's fashion's great recluse.
Whispers tales of years gone by,
As it watches trends fly high.

So if ever you should glance,
At a gem in quiet chance,
Know it brings a wink and sigh,
A lifetime's worth of 'Oh my!'

Whispers of Gold and Gem

A golden pin with silly flair,
Whispers secrets to the air.
In parties, it steals the show,
With a wink and cheeky glow.

Once a lucky charm was worn,
Now it snickers, slightly torn.
Upon a scarf, it takes a stand,
Like a star that's slightly bland.

Each diamond, a gleaming jest,
Competing with a silly vest.
In a world of glitz and glow,
It laughs softly, 'I told you so!'

Amid the glimmer, hear it tease,
'I'm timeless, darling, if you please!'
With every twinkle, it's a hit,
A charm that makes you laugh a bit!

Adornment's Silent Saga

A vintage pin with stories stacked,
In dusty corners, once it cracked.
With peacock colors, old and shy,
Winks at passersby up high.

Once it held a diva's grace,
Now it sports a silly face.
'Twas a knight's shining brave affair,
Now just rests without a care.

In fashion's vault, it lost its fight,
Yet still chuckles day and night.
Stitching memories, soft and sweet,
With every wear, its tales repeat.

If you seek the funny things,
Where laughter loops and joy still sings,
Find that pin with diamonds set,
It's got jokes you won't forget!

Memories Cloaked in Accessories

In a box what treasures lay,
An accessory with much to say.
A silver leaf, once finely dressed,
Now just giggles, quite a jest.

Each time it's pinned, it sings a tune,
Of fashion faux pas and afternoon.
Worn atop a frilly shirt,
"It's just a pin!" with playful flirt.

Gather 'round for tales so bold,
Of past parties, laughter told.
In the hall of this fabled charm,
It wraps itself in quirky arm.

So raise a glass to stories spun,
In the glow of the setting sun.
With every clip, a joyful plea,
"Don't forget to laugh with me!"

A Legacy in Lusters

In a drawer so deep and wide,
Lies a trinket, polished, dignified.
Once a gift, now a joke,
Worn by a pooch, all tailored bespoke.

With sparkles bright, it twinkled at night,
On his collar, a comical sight.
People stopped, they laughed and sighed,
'Is that a dog? Or a fashion guide?'

But oh, that charm holds tales galore,
Of fancy parties and even more.
A legacy in lusters bright,
Whispering secrets of canine delight.

As it lies now, neglected and free,
Worn by the dog who just had to be.
A memory wrapped in glimmer and grin,
In every sparkle, the laughter begins.

The Subtle Mark of Beauty

A golden pin sat on a shelf,
Whispering tales of itself.
Dusted off for a night out,
'Look at me!' it seemed to shout.

Worn to brunch with friends so dear,
Making muffins look austere.
Yet it clashed with coffee, how absurd,
A fashion faux pas, oh, how it stirred!

As it danced in the afternoon sun,
Reflecting light, causing a run.
The subtle mark of beauty thrives,
In humor found, where laughter drives.

Now tucked away in a case so bright,
Awaiting days for more delight.
Who knew a pin could bring such cheer?
In silliness, its charm is clear.

A Pin's Poignant Journey

Once upon a time, so spry,
A pin took flight, oh me, oh my!
To a wedding, it flew with grace,
Got stuck in cake, made quite the face.

Friends gathered 'round, it sparked delight,
'Is that the cake, or a pin in flight?'
Laughter erupted, a funny feast,
And thus our pin became a beast.

From the sleeve of a groom, to the cake's sweet heart,
On a joyous journey, it played its part.
With every mishap, it shone so bright,
A pin's poignant journey, laughter took flight.

Now rests in a box, tales untold,
Of mishaps and spills, and laughter bold.
Someday it will shine once more with glee,
When laughter calls, just wait and see!

Encased in Gleam

A pendant bright, encased in gleam,
Hugging memories, like a dream.
Once adorned a hat, or so they say,
Now a paperweight, in a funny way.

It tells of dances and parties past,
When every wink was a blast.
But now it sits, quite out of reach,
Awaiting news from the fashion breach.

Did that style rage, or was it just a phase?
With glittering eyes, in a baffling daze.
Encased in gleam, it craves some flair,
To glitter once more, but no one's aware.

Yet underneath the dust and the gloom,
Lies a spark, waiting to bloom.
So here's to moments, both silly and bright,
For in laughter, there's always light.

Emblems of Unspoken Love

In a drawer, they lie so still,
Whispers of the heart, yet to spill.
A sparkly friend with no loud shout,
What secrets hide without a doubt?

They twinkle bright, they dance with glee,
Telling tales of you and me.
In laughter's glow, they softly tease,
Unseen stories that aim to please.

With silly smiles and shy delight,
They sneak around in the soft moonlight.
A bond expressed without a word,
In glimmers caught, their love is stirred.

Oh, for a laugh and wink we'll share,
In joy, they elevate the air.
These splendid gems, no need for fuss,
In playful hugs, they ride the bus.

The Serene Language of Adornments

Sitting in boxes, they stir and laugh,
A jeweled crowd in a silly staff.
They jingle and jangle, quite the show,
Of love in metal, a charming glow.

With every twirl, they spin a tale,
In glittered dreams, they never fail.
From frosty pearls to a zany clip,
They wear each story, a friendship's grip.

On dullest days, they light the scene,
Turning awkward into routine.
Subtle nudges, a sly little grin,
They know the joy that's tucked within.

A wink, a nod, they keep it light,
In quiet corners, shining bright.
With gentle charm, they'll crack a jest,
A gleaming force, they're simply the best.

Music in Metal and Stone

In a sparkle-symphony, they gleefully chime,
Whirling gossip of a grand good time.
With tunes of laughter, they sway about,
No need for words, just giggles and clout.

Their messages float on a shimmered breeze,
Tickling earlobes like playful tease.
Each glint and glimmer holds a dance,
Inviting hearts to take a chance.

In playful gatherings, they have a ball,
Making each moment a joyous call.
With every sparkle, a note is played,
A melody of cheer, intertwined and laid.

So gather round with a playful cheer,
Let's celebrate all we hold dear.
In shiny tokens, we find our way,
Singing laughter in the light of day.

Trinkets of Time's Embrace

Tick-tock trinkets spin and dance,
In their tiny world, they take a chance.
Every tick, every clink is a giggle,
In their grand tales, they twist and wiggle.

Oh, the tales they could tell, who knows?
Of far-off lands and secret shows.
With every glance, they wink with charm,
Keeping moments safe and warm.

From brooches bold to clips so neat,
Each painted smile is a little treat.
In the treasure chest, they jive about,
While we laugh together, there's never doubt.

So give a cheer for these quirky friends,
With silly stories that never end.
In the realm of adornments, let's confide,
In every sparkle, pure joy won't hide.

The Poetry of Precious Pins

In a drawer of forgotten flair,
Lie pins with tales beyond compare.
One wore a hat, so grand, so wide,
While another pretended to be a bride.

A ladybug laughs with jeweled glee,
Next to a fish that just won't flee.
Each tiny clasp has a silly scheme,
In a world where laughter reigns supreme.

The sassy squirrel winks with pride,
As the flower flirts, its petals slide.
Oh, how they bicker for the limelight,
In the whimsical shadows of the night.

The pins gather stories, oh what a feast,
From the dusk till dawn, they never cease.
Whispers of fashion, fun to unpin,
With each tiny tale, let the laughter begin!

Threads of History Woven

Stitches of yore in laughter's weave,
Whimsical tales that never leave.
A needle's dance, a thread's delight,
Each loop and twist a humorous sight.

From past to present, they giggle along,
A tapestry woven of mischief and song.
Patches of joy in a fabric so bright,
Whispering tales in the soft starlight.

Oh, the tales from the couch so worn,
Where seamstress dreams and laughter were born.
A patchwork quilt with quirks to unveil,
Each seam a chuckle, each fold a tale.

In stitches and knots, the stories grow,
Playing hide and seek in the threads below.
They may be quiet, but oh, take a peek —
These stitched-up secrets love to speak!

Enigma of the Enamel

In a world where colors play tag,
Enamels glimmer with a giggly rag.
A shiny cat, a dancing shoe,
Each enamel piece has a whimsical view.

A pinning puzzle, a playful game,
Which one's the thief? Do they all have name?
The laughing pumpkin tricks the sly fox,
And a rainbow fish just loves to box.

A coat of paints, like jests on the wall,
Each hue tells a riddle, each color a call.
With smiles that shine from lives long gone,
These cheeky trinkets will carry on.

In enamel whispers, the joy is loud,
Secrets of laughter, they're surely proud.
They sparkle and shimmer with giggles galore,
And embrace the silliness forevermore!

Tales in a Twinkle

In the gleam of a twinkle, a story unfolds,
Of playful adventures and treasures untold.
A starlet pin winks with a sly little grin,
As a crescent moon giggles at the mischief within.

Each flicker and shimmer holds raucous delight,
Telling tales of laughter in the quiet of night.
The buttons all chatter, each bead has a laugh,
As they gather together for a joyous craft.

A diamond giggles, a pearl does a jig,
While the emerald sings songs that are big.
They dance in the light, with sparkles so bright,
In the theater of whimsy, they steal the night.

Oh, what a circus, these gems and their charms,
With each little twinkle, the humor disarms.
In a twinkling minute, their tales take flight,
Bringing joy to the world, a whimsical sight!

In the Shadow of Sparkle

In a drawer, tucked away tight,
Lies a pin, shining so bright.
It whispers tales of fashion gone wrong,
Claiming it danced all night long.

With a wobble and jig, it takes the lead,
Remembers the days of pom-pom bead.
Feathers and frills, it wore with flair,
Catching the eyes, and folks would stare.

When the wind blew, oh what a sight,
It twirled and spiraled like a kite!
With laughter echoing, it perseveres,
A relic of joy, through the years.

So next time you find one all alone,
Give it a spin, let it be known.
For every glimmer hides a jest,
In the stories where pins do rest.

Echoes of Elegance

Once was a clasp, a bit askew,
It fancied itself a royal view.
With pearls and glitter stuck on tight,
It laughed at the mirror, day and night.

A fashionista's gaffe, indeed,
It glittered in sunlight, took the lead.
"Oh darling, can't you see my charm?"
"Or is it just the cat's alarm?"

It cursed the days of stiff-backed wear,
Wishing for fun, a little flair.
Under the couch, it rolled with glee,
Hosting a party for the lost keys!

So don't toss it out, give it a chance,
There's magic in its silly dance.
For every misfit, shines a joke,
In echoes of elegance, joy awoke.

A Pin of Timeless Tales

A pin once perched on a frumpy dress,
Claiming it brought elegance, no less.
But like a mime, it told no lies,
As it chuckled low and rolled its eyes.

It creaked with tales from a club of three,
A badge of honor for the kind of spree.
Crafted for laughter, it took its stand,
Worn by a queen who'd lost her hand!

In a box, it sits, dreaming big,
Hoping to be the next fashion gig.
As a laugh-enducer, it holds the key,
To priceless joy, as all can see.

So if you spy it, give it a twirl,
This little pin could change your world.
For in every laughter, there's a tale,
A pin of memories that will prevail.

Shimmering Threads of Nostalgia

Once there was a pin woven tight,
Sparkling threads of pure delight.
It savored the past, relished each chance,
Spinning yarns like a grand old dance.

Fighting the frumpy with all its might,
It snickered at collars, oh what a sight!
A treasure once lost at a fun fair,
Came back to shine, in timeless flair.

With stories of picnics and pies in the air,
Each glittering gem declared, "I was there!"
In bonkers bow ties and wild costume swaps,
Nostalgia winks as the laughing stops.

So let it remind you, as you wear it proud,
Memories shimmer, they're never too loud.
For in the light, a story may pierce,
Shimmering threads weave joy, oh so fierce.

Reflections in Ribbons

In the drawer, a treasure lies,
A twist of fate made from bright ties.
With sequins and threads in a playful spin,
Who knew this piece held such a grin?

Each ribbon dances with a little flair,
Whispering tales of parties rare.
It once adorned a hat so grand,
Now it laughs, resting in my hand.

A frog once leaped upon this crest,
Claimed it's regal, claimed it's best.
But really, it's just an old surprise,
Dressed up for life in a sweet disguise.

Yet, here we sit, a pair of friends,
Me with my quirks and you with bends.
Together we chuckle in muted delight,
Who knew such fashion could be this light?

Echoes in Everyday Elegance

At the gala, the crowd did cheer,
A flash of color, it's finally here!
It sparkled bright, but oh what a tease,
Made the catwalk feel like a breeze.

With each step, it plotted a prank,
To steal some hearts, give wit a yank.
As it jiggled and jived, a twinkling jest,
Even the fashion snobs felt impressed.

But when all was dim and silent spun,
It whispered secrets of each little pun.
A feather, a pearl, wrapped in a twist,
Not just a jewel, but part of the list.

In daily life, it winks like a friend,
A laugh from the past, won't this trend bend?
Even a blouse can wear a surprise,
In whispers of laughter, elegance lies!

A Story Beneath the Surface

Look closely now, it's hard to find,
A shimmer here, a little unwind.
It's not hiding gold, nor secret lore,
Just giggles and shadows, a little more.

Once a sailor with dreams so bold,
He thought it would fetch a fortune untold.
But it took a trip through hats and tears,
Now all it holds are snickers and cheers.

Underneath layers of sparkly sheen,
Lie memories of mischief, fun, and keen.
A wink, a nod, from days gone by,
Oh, the tales it tells—if only it could cry!

With a flip and a twist, it starts to sing,
Of toast and laughter, and widening rings.
Each facet bright with stories to share,
In the sparkle of life, we all find our flair!

The Jewel's Secret Life

In a corner, where no one peeks,
This gem chats softly, sharing tweaks.
A comrade to socks, it finds them neat,
Bumping the blender, oh what a feat!

It thinks it's royal and gives a wink,
To lonely spools that never think.
From attic dreams to sock drawer schemes,
It spins a yarn with mischievous gleams.

Last Sunday, it tried to dance and sway,
But tripped on the rug, oh what a display!
Yet there it lay, giggling bright,
In a world of dullness, it brought the light.

So here's to jewels with stories to tell,
Who flourish in closets, oh quite well.
Each stitch, each twinkle, holds a jest,
In their hidden lives, they are truly blessed!

www.ingramcontent.com/pod-product-compliance
Lightning Source LLC
Chambersburg PA
CBHW070304120526
44590CB00017B/2559